First American edition 2013.
First UK edition 2012.

Tharpa Publications US Office
47 Sweeney Road
Glen Spey, NY
12737, USA

Tharpa Publications UK Office
Conishead Priory
Ulverston, Cumbria
LA12 9QQ, UK

Tharpa Publications is part of the
New Kadampa Tradition – International Kadampa Buddhist Union (NKT-IKBU).
Tharpa has offices around the world and Tharpa books are published in most major languages.

Text and Illustrations
© New Kadampa Tradition – International Kadampa Buddhist Union 2012, 2013

Library of Congress Control Number: 2012955584

ISBN: 978-1-61606-021-3 – paperback

Set in Candara by Tharpa Publications.

Paper supplied from well-managed forests and other controlled sources, and certified in accordance with the rules of the Forest Stewardship Council.

The Story of Angulimala

GESHE KELSANG GYATSO

Buddhism for Children Level One

THARPA PUBLICATIONS
US • UK • CANADA
AUSTRALIA • ASIA

The Story of Angulimala

Many years ago Buddha Shakyamuni became enlightened under the Bodhi Tree at Bodh Gaya in India.

Later the gods Brahma and Indra asked him to teach everyone how to become enlightened.

So Buddha Shakyamuni taught the people of this world how to overcome suffering and problems, how to be calm and peaceful, and how to be loving and kind towards each other.

Buddha traveled from place to place, and whenever he stopped he would teach people about love, compassion, and wisdom.

He taught them how to overcome their daily problems such as worrying, arguing, feeling ill or tired, feeling upset when we don't get what we want or when we have to do something we don't want to do.

Buddha taught people that we don't need to worry about all these little problems. Instead we can use our life to love and help others, to develop wisdom, and to become enlightened, so that we can always feel happy and can help others to feel happy too.

One day Buddha arrived in a village that appeared to be deserted. All the huts seemed to be empty. There was a great silence everywhere. Then a young woman ran out from one of the huts sobbing. She said to Buddha,

> "*O dear Lord Buddha, please do not walk in this area, there is a madman running wild. His name is Angulimala, he carries an axe and has already killed 999 people! Dear Buddha, please do not stay in this place, it is too dangerous.*"

Buddha stayed very calm, he smiled at the woman in a kindly way and said,

> "*Thank you for your concern, but you don't need to worry about me, I'll be fine.*"

Buddha continued to walk along the empty road. Then the woman ran out in front of him once again and pleaded with him,

" *O Buddha, please, please turn back.*
He is so dangerous
he will kill you! "

Buddha gently told her not to worry, and then he continued walking.

After a while Buddha became aware
of a loud noise in the distance.

He looked back and saw a man
a long way behind making a lot
of noise and clashing his weapons.
He could see that this man was
wearing a necklace of fingers
around his neck!

Buddha stopped walking and used his
miracle powers so that no matter how fast
Angulimala tried to run towards Buddha he
could not catch up.

He tried harder and harder until
he was exhausted and then finally
he shouted to Buddha,

" *Stop! Stop!* "

Buddha replied,

" *Angulimala, I have already
stopped, you are the one
who needs to stop.* "

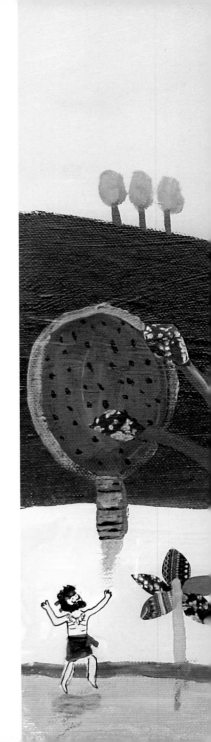

He tried to hurl his axe at Buddha, but he could not do it!

He tried to grab Buddha with his
bare hands,
but he could not do it!

Buddha then gently told Angulimala to calm down and to sit down in front of him. Just sitting in Buddha's presence Angulimala felt very special and peaceful. For the first time in a long, long time he felt different—he stopped feeling angry. He sat looking at Buddha for a long time and he was amazed by him. He thought,

"*This is the first time I have met someone who is not frightened of me.*"

Then Angulimala with a calm mind asked Buddha,

"*What did you mean when you said, 'I have already stopped, you are the one who needs to stop'?*"

Buddha replied,

"*I am telling you that I have already stopped harmful actions a long time ago, so I am free from fear towards everyone including you. Now you need to stop harmful actions so that you will be free from future suffering and fear.*"

Angulimala deeply appreciated Buddha's teaching and he made a promise in front of Buddha to stop harming others, including killing. He began to understand how terrible it is to be angry. Anger harms ourself and it harms others, and it is the main cause of all the conflicts and wars in this world.

Angulimala did not want to be angry any more. He threw away his weapons and necklace of fingers and he felt a huge sense of relief and peace in his heart.

Gradually, over time, Angulimala transformed himself taking Buddha as his example. In this way he changed his life and learned to be kind, wise, and compassionate towards everyone.

This story shows you that everyone, even those who experience a miserable life due to having very rough minds and having performed harmful actions, can transform their life into a peaceful, happy, and meaningful life through receiving Buddha's blessings.

About the Author

Geshe Kelsang Gyatso, or Geshe-la as he is affectionately known by his students, is a world-renowned Buddhist meditation master who has pioneered the introduction of modern Buddhism into contemporary society.

Through his personal example and his public teachings and writings he demonstrates how everyone, whether Buddhist or non-Buddhist, can learn to become wiser and more compassionate by following the advice of Buddha.

Geshe Kelsang is the founder of the International Kadampa Schools Project, which was inaugurated in September 2012 with the opening of the first International Kadampa Primary School in Derbyshire, England.

Children meditating at Kadampa Primary School Derbyshire, England.

The *Buddhism for Children* series:

The **Buddhism for Children** series invites children to make a journey of self-discovery and self-improvement to help them realize their full potential.

The purpose is not to convert them to Buddhism but simply to show how everyone, Buddhist or non-Buddhist, can learn something from the teachings of Buddha.

These books address the reader in a mature fashion, using the life and teachings of Buddha as a basis for exploring many of the issues and concerns that confront children today.

Although these books are written principally for children, anyone who wants a clear explanation of the essence of Buddhism and how it applies to modern living will benefit greatly from reading them.

For more books, audio, and artwork on Buddhism and Meditation visit: **www.tharpa.com**

Buddhism for Children Level 1
The Story of Angulimala

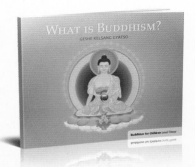

Buddhism for Children Level 2
The Story of Buddha

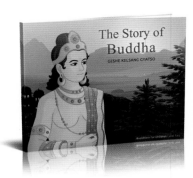

Buddhism for Children Level 3
What is Buddhism?

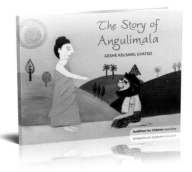

Buddhism for Children Level 4
What is Meditation?

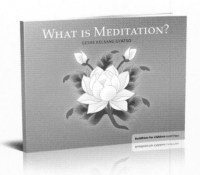